Project 7-11

Developing

Maths

Book 2

Ann Douglas, Valerie Ellis and Jim Boucher

for 8-9 year olds

Letts

Here is my picture of Pamela Polygon.

What shapes have I used?

► Ask an adult or look in a dictionary for any spellings you are not sure of.

Head _____

Eyes _____

Nose _____

Mouth _____

Neck _____

Skirt _____

Bow _____

Hands _____

Shoulders _____

Body _____

Arms _____

Legs _____

Feet _____

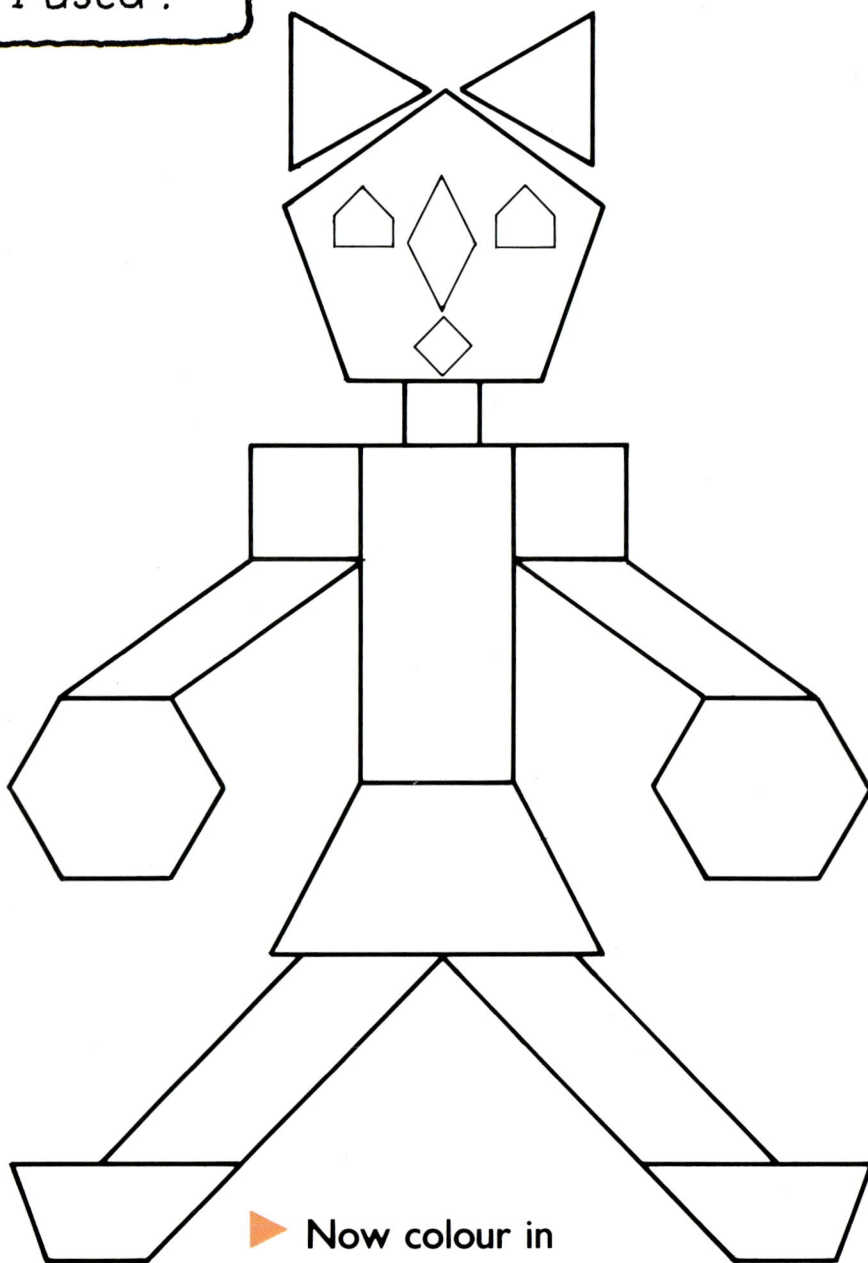

► Now colour in Pamela Polygon.

Now it's your turn!
Draw Peter Polygon and his dog,
Patch. Use a ruler to help you.

Polygons
have straight
sides.

PETER POLYGON

PATCH

▶ Now colour in
Peter Polygon and Patch.

3

I've trapped 3 squares.

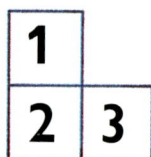

So have I !

$\frac{1}{2}$ 1 $\frac{1}{2}$
2

1
2 3

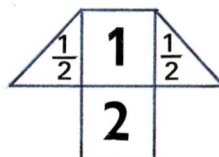

I trapped two full squares and two half squares, to make three squares altogether.

► How many squares are trapped inside each of these shapes?
Emma has done the first one for you.

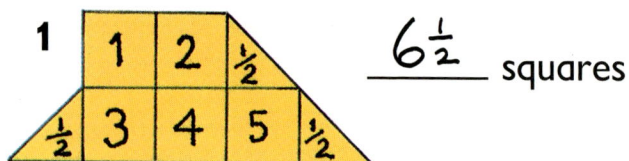

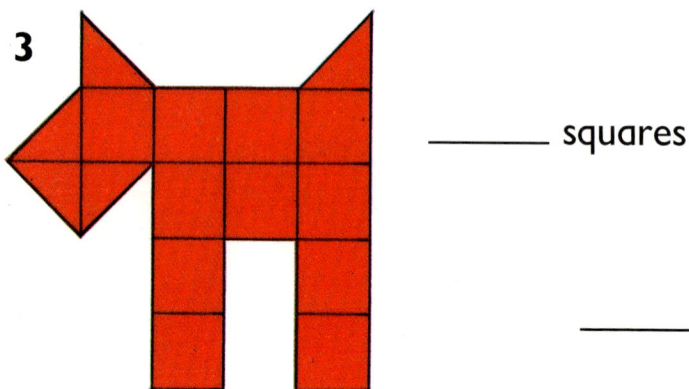

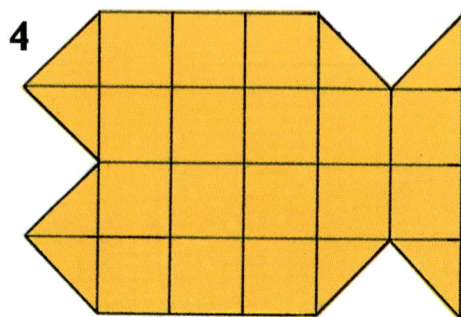

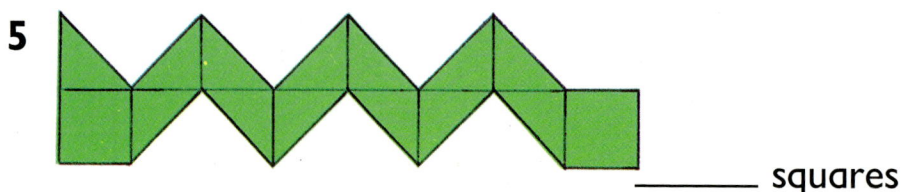

1

| 1 | 2 | $\frac{1}{2}$ |
| $\frac{1}{2}$ 3 | 4 | 5 $\frac{1}{2}$ |

$6\frac{1}{2}$ squares

2 _____ squares

3 _____ squares

4 _____ squares

5 _____ squares

How many different shapes can you make which trap 5½ squares? Draw them below.
I've done three for you.

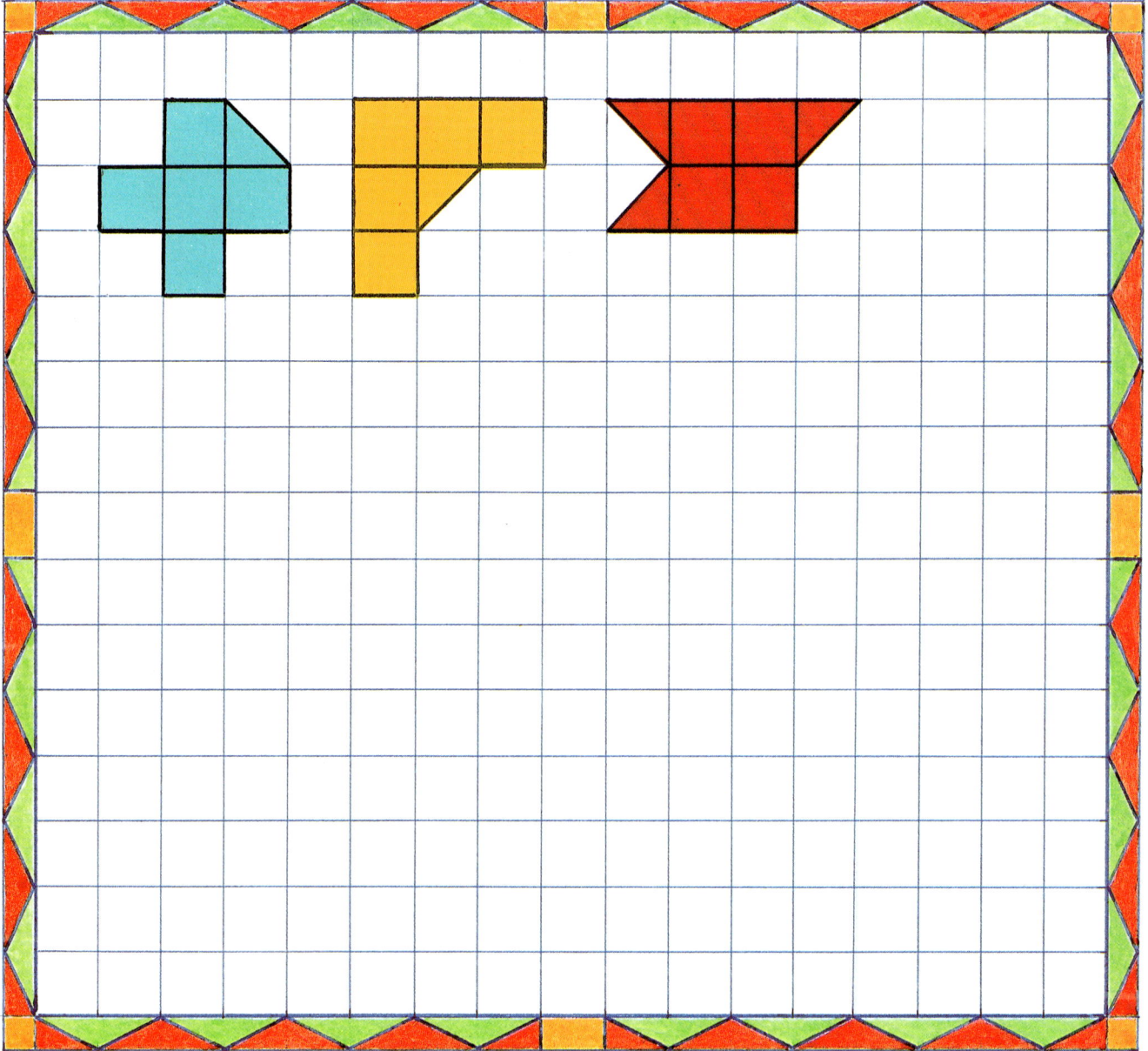

If you managed to find 10, we think you're ACE!

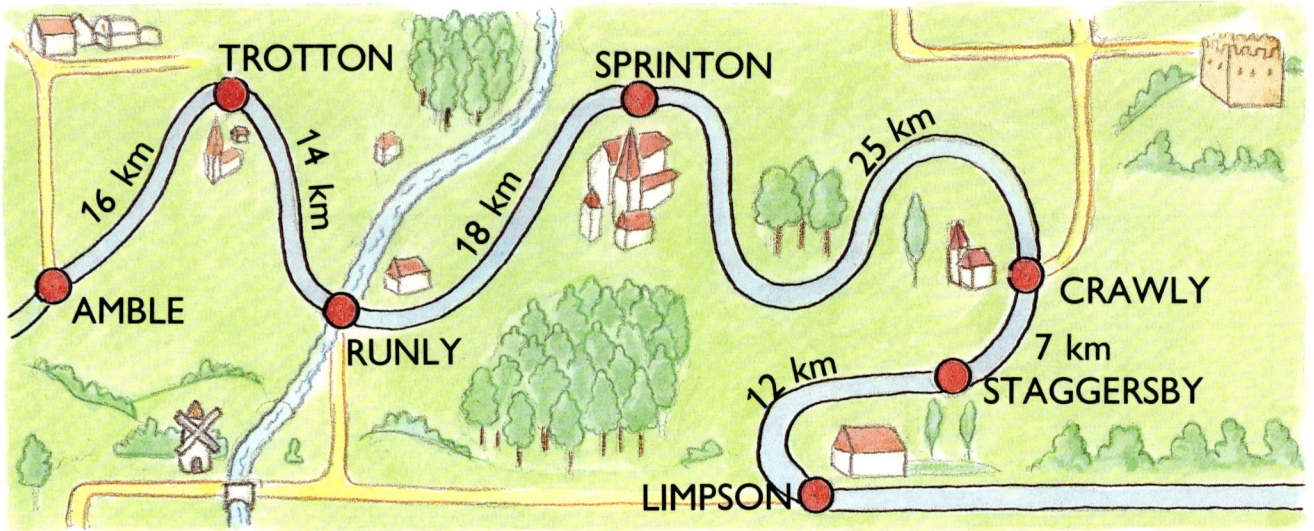

▶ Use the map above to find how far it is:

1 From Sprinton to Crawly _____ km.

2 From Trotton to Sprinton _____ km.

3 From Staggersby to Sprinton _____ km.

4 From Runly to Crawly _____ km.

5 From Sprinton to Limpson and back to Crawly _____ km.

km stands for kilometre.

You may use your calculator or work these out on a piece of paper.

The signposts below are **somewhere** along the road
from Amble to Limpson.
One of the distances is missing from each signpost.

▶ Use the map to help you find the missing distances.

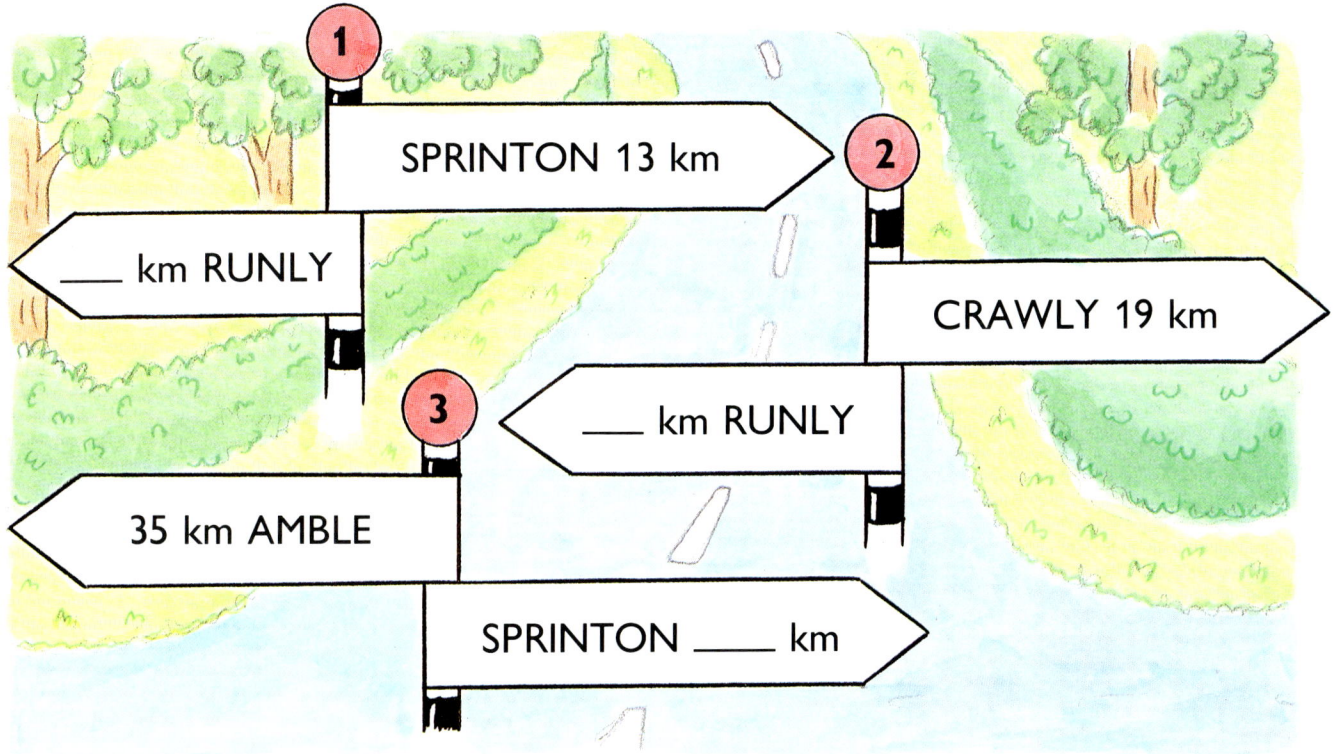

1 SPRINTON 13 km

2 CRAWLY 19 km

___ km RUNLY

___ km RUNLY

3

35 km AMBLE

SPRINTON ___ km

The name of a town is missing from each of the
signposts below.

▶ Use the map to help you find the missing names.

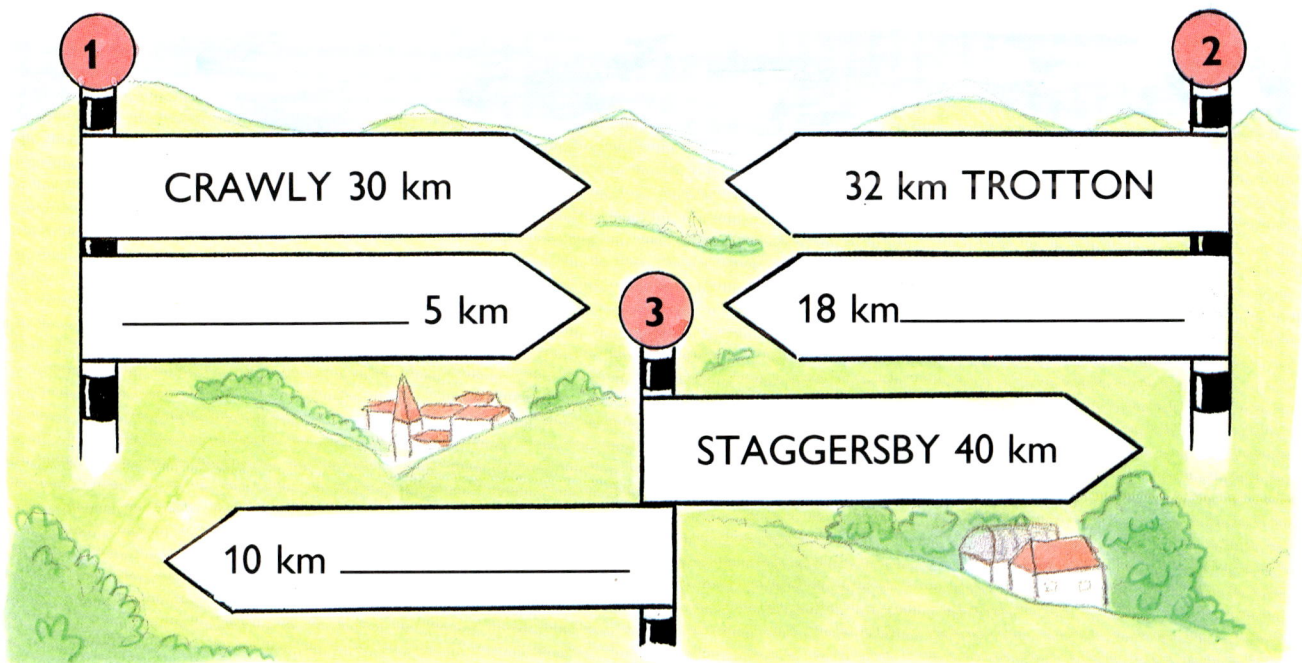

1 CRAWLY 30 km

2 32 km TROTTON

___ 5 km

3 18 km ___

STAGGERSBY 40 km

10 km ___

4 At sixes and sevens

► Complete Spider's Menu Card.

SPIDER'S MENU

1 fly .... 6 legs
2 flies .... _____ legs
3 flies .... _____ legs
4 flies .... _____ legs
5 flies .... _____ legs
6 flies .... _____ legs
7 flies .... _____ legs
8 flies .... _____ legs
9 flies .... _____ legs
10 flies .... _____ legs

► Join the labels to the correct suitcases.

4 weeks
1 week
7 weeks
3 weeks

63 days
21 days
7 days

70 days
35 days

28 days
56 days

14 days
42 days
49 days

5 weeks
6 weeks

10 weeks
9 weeks
A fortnight
8 weeks

Mark was looking at the **units** digits in his 6 times table.

$6 \times 1 = 6$
$6 \times 2 = 12$
$6 \times 3 = 18$

He started to join these points on the circle in order.

Can you finish my sixes circle pattern?

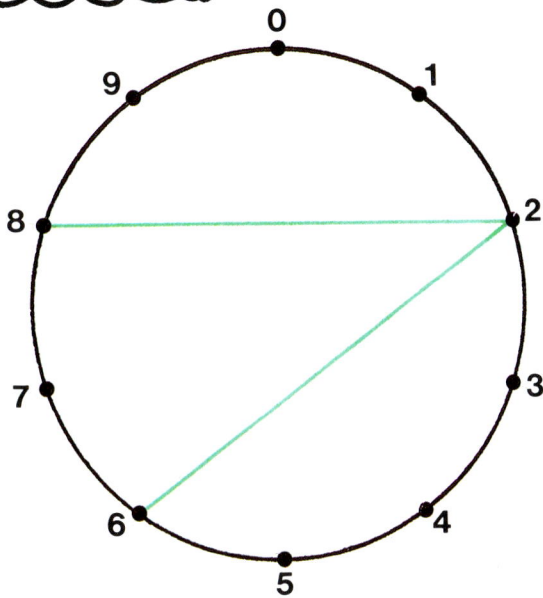

Mark wondered whether the **units** digits from his 7 times table would also make a pattern.

$7 \times 1 = 7$
$7 \times 2 = 14$
$7 \times 3 = 21$

Finish my sevens circle pattern.

Hint: You will need to go up to 7×11 to complete the pattern.

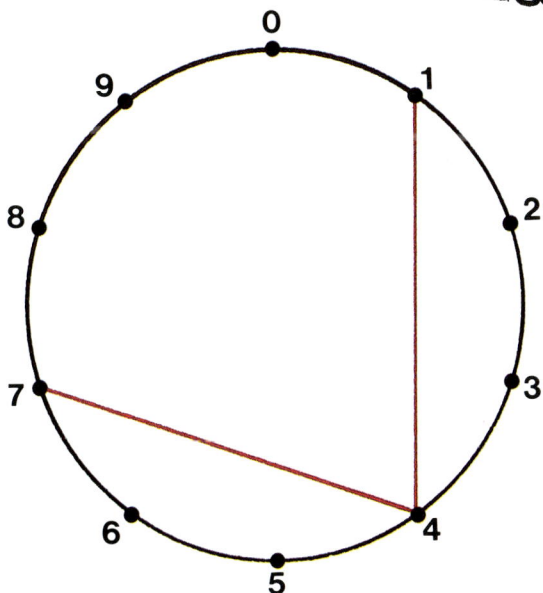

▶ Now colour in your circle patterns.

5 How do you measure up?

I think you've grown more than me this year, Gary.

Yes, I think I'm begining to shoot up now.

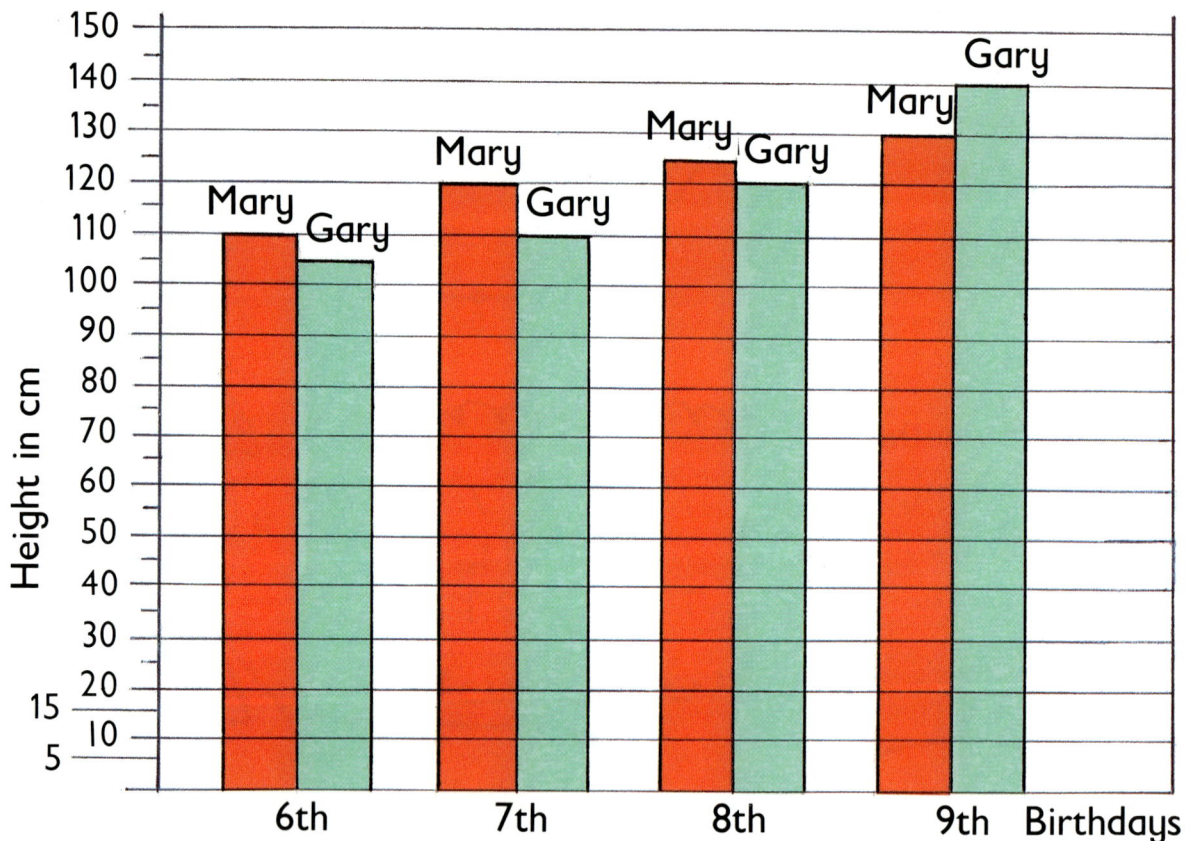

▶ Look at the chart and answer these questions:

1 How tall was Mary on her 8th birthday? _____ cm

2 How tall was Gary when he was six? _____ cm

3 Who was the taller when they were seven years old? _____

4 How much taller than Gary was Mary when they were eight years old? _____ cm

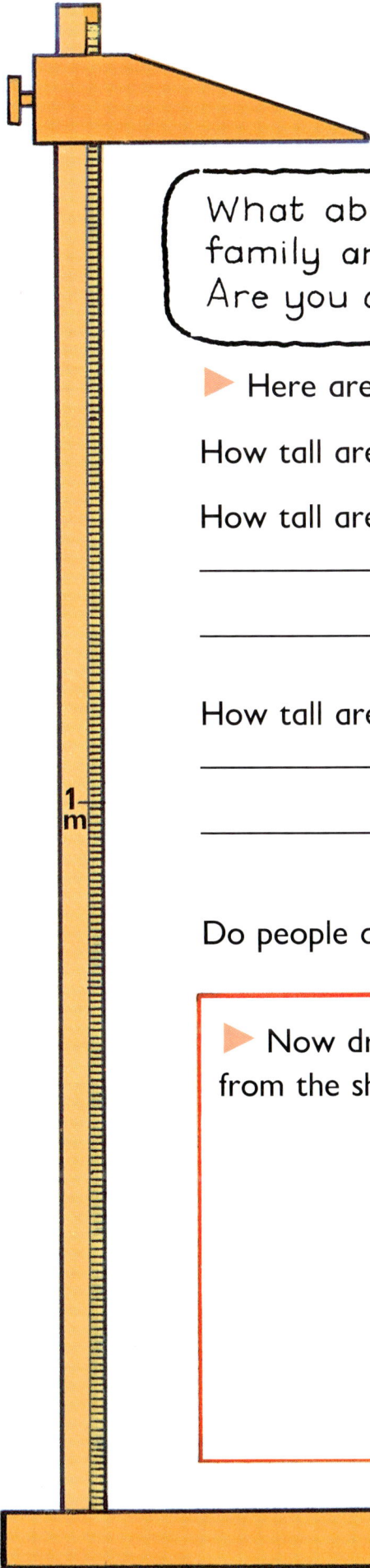

What about you and your family and friends? Are you all still growing?

▶ Here are some questions for you:

How tall are you? _____ cm

How tall are the other members of your family?

_____

_____

How tall are your friends?

_____

_____

Do people always keep on growing? _____

▶ Now draw a picture to show everyone you have asked, from the shortest to the tallest.

1 m

6 Tessellating shapes

Some shapes fit together without leaving any spaces and some don't. When they do fit together they tessellate. Look at these shapes!

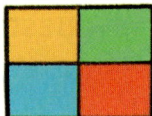 

▶ Which shapes tessellate?   Tick those that do tessellate.

By moving a piece of a shape from one place and adding it somewhere else, you can make a tessellating picture. Look at these!

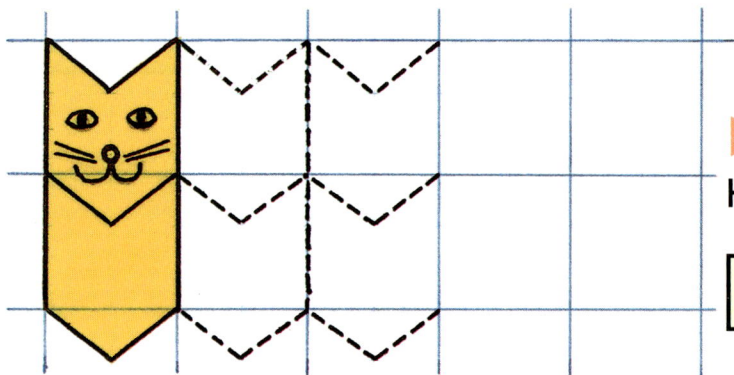

▶ Finish making the faces. How many faces are there?

☐ faces

▶ Finish drawing the dogs. How many are there?

☐ dogs

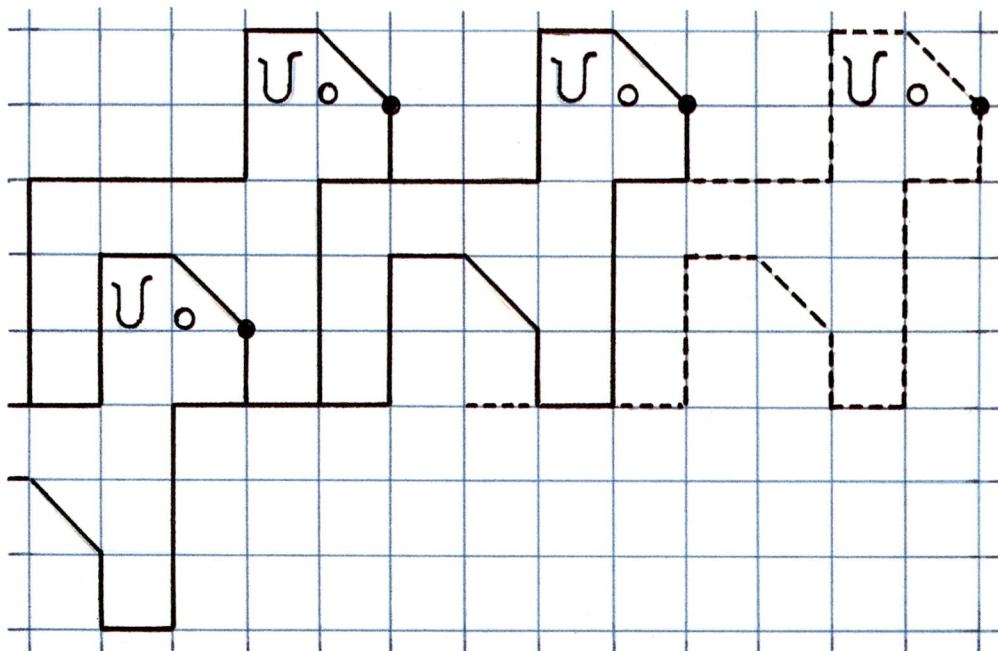

Here are some more pictures for you to finish.

Colour in the ducks and the fishes when you have finished them.

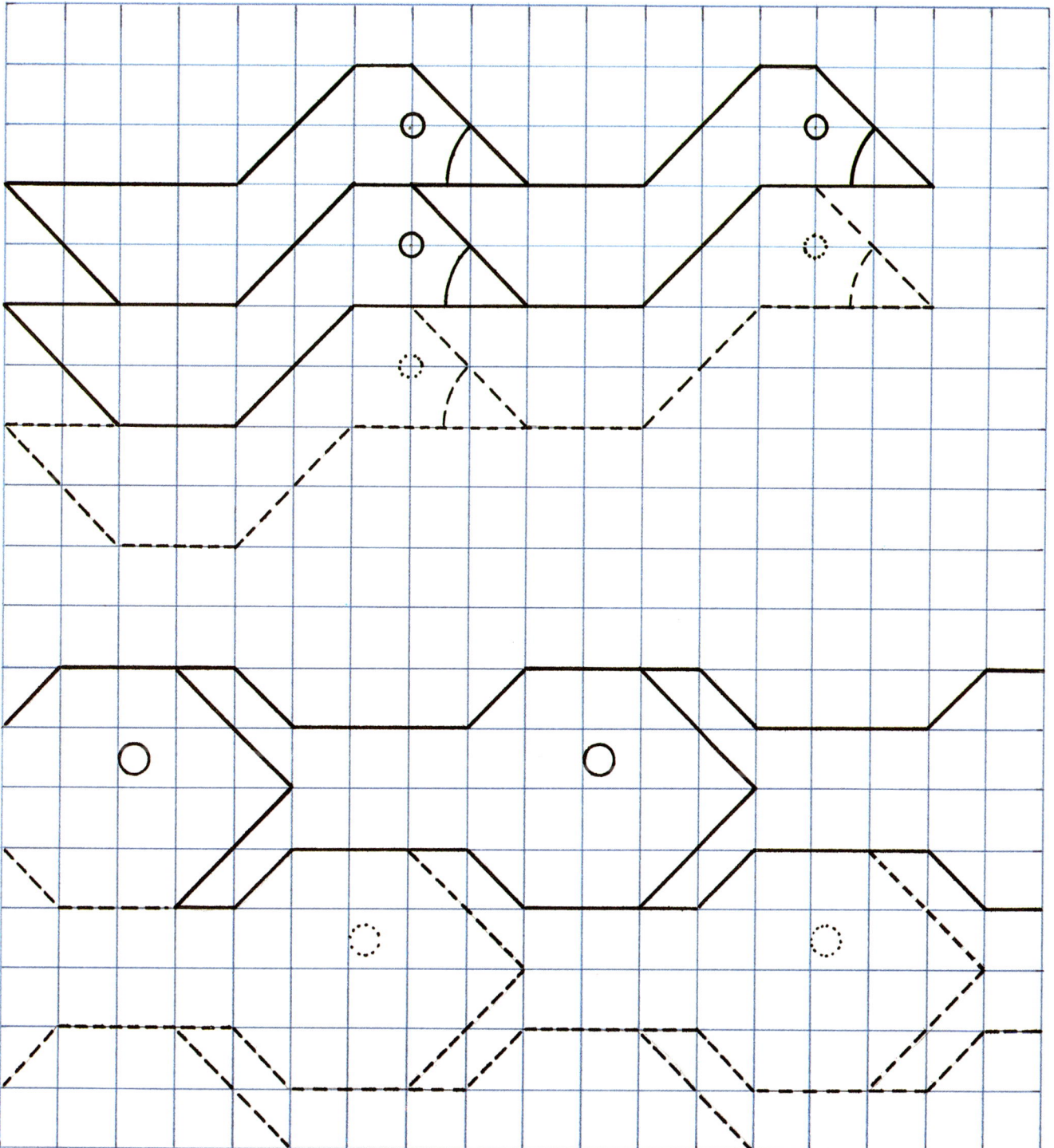

▶ Have a game of dominoes with a friend.
Make sure you follow the rules.
Cut out and use the set
from the back cover.

▶ Sort out the dominoes which have
5s or 6s on them.

Can you place your dominoes to match this pattern?

6	1						
3	5	5					
	3	6		1	5		
5	6	6	6	5	2	6	BLANK
4	4	6		5	BLANK	5	6
						5	2

Tick if you managed it ☐ .

Here is a domino trick you can play on a friend.

Ask your friend to choose any domino.... without showing it to you.

Tell your friend to

—Multiply the larger number by 5.
—Add 8.
—Multiply by 2.
—Add the smaller number on the domino.

Tell me that number.

$4 \times 5 = 20$
$20 + 8 = 28$
$28 \times 2 = 56$
$56 + 1 = 57$

Fifty - seven.

Now you subtract 16 from that number...
$57 - 16 = 41$.

How did he do it?

Your two numbers are FOUR and ONE.

Mine is the <u>shortest</u> distance all the way round.

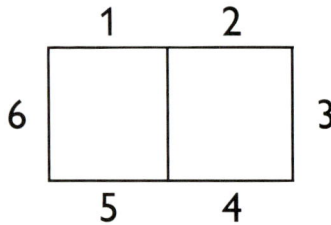

```
    1    2
   ┌────┬────┐
 6 │    │    │ 3
   └────┴────┘
    5    4
```

Mine is the <u>longest</u> distance all the way round.

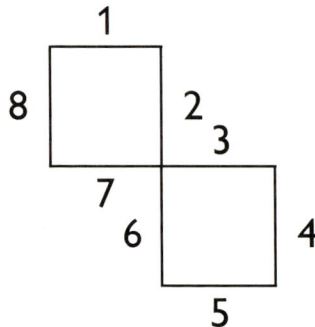

```
    1
   ┌────┐
 8 │    │ 2
   └────┤ 3
      7 ┌────┐
      6 │    │ 4
        └────┘
          5
```

▶ Copy and cut out these six square tiles.

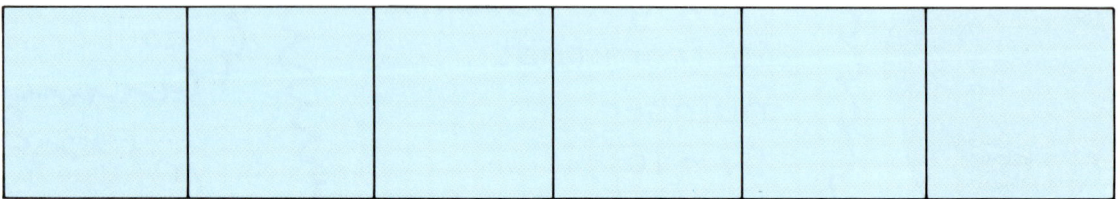

So now you will have six squares.

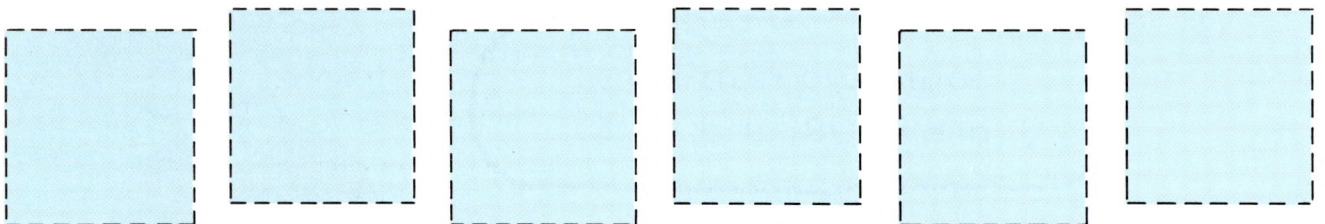

Use this space to find the shortest and longest distance all the way round the tiles.

Number of square tiles	Shortest distance all the way round Units	Longest distance all the way round Units
1		
2	6	
3		
4		
5		20
6		

Can you see a pattern here?

What about here?

17

9 Rangoli patterns

Rangoli patterns can be made by joining the dots on a grid and filling the sections with coloured sand.

Here are some for you to finish and colour with pencils or felt-tips.

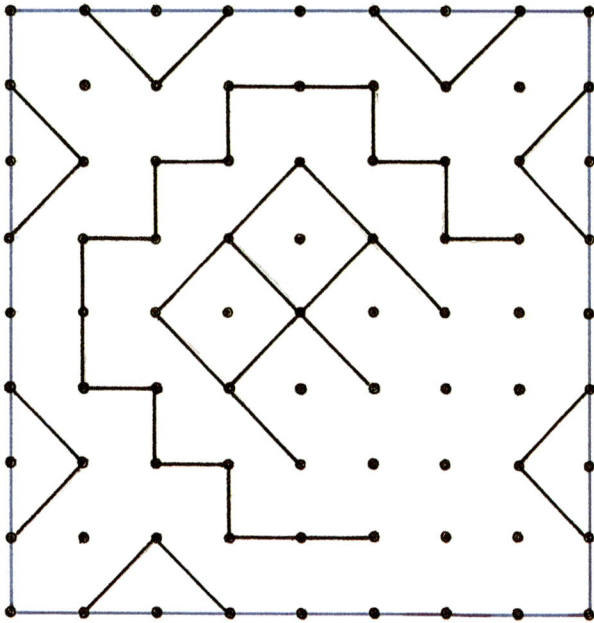

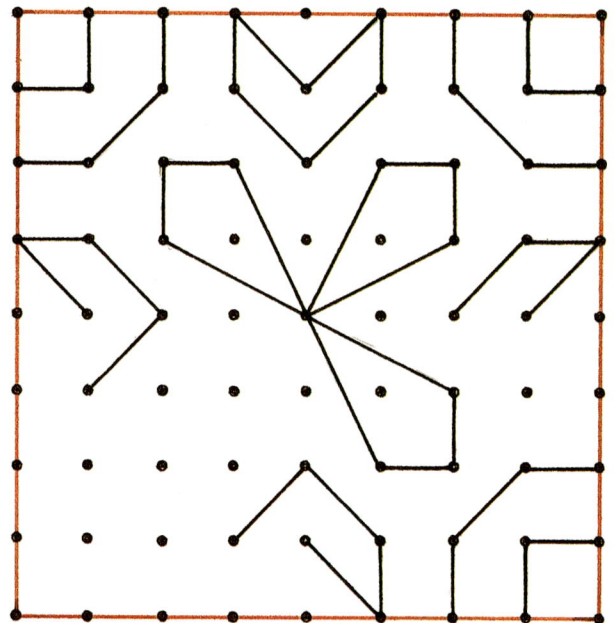

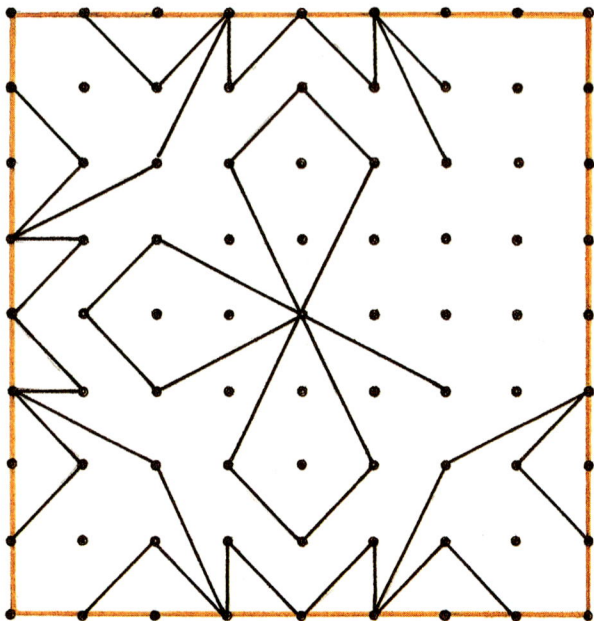

► Now draw and colour some of your own Rangoli patterns.

You can make them as simple or as complicated as you wish, but they must be symmetrical.

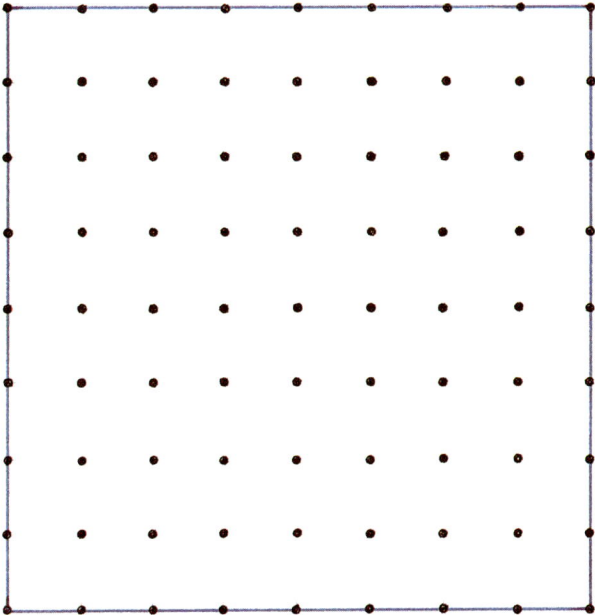

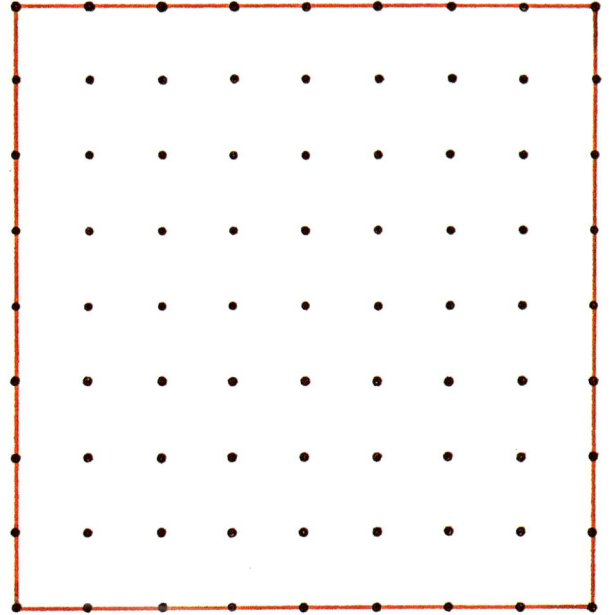

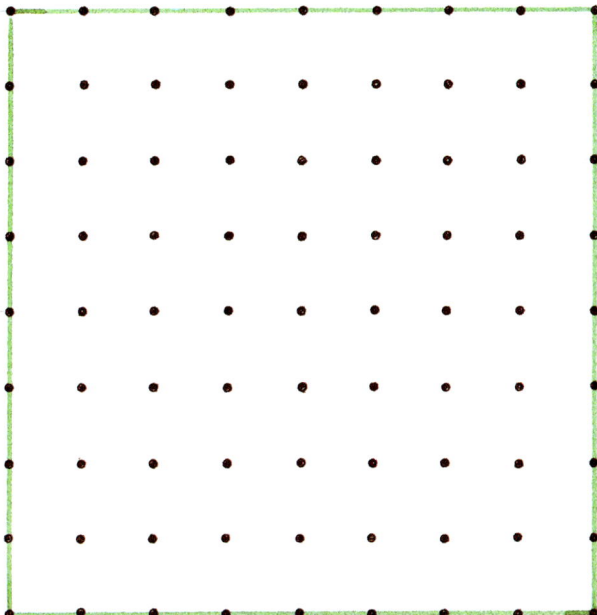

I think I'm Rangoli-eyed!

Supersquares

Hamid made some squares with his tiles.

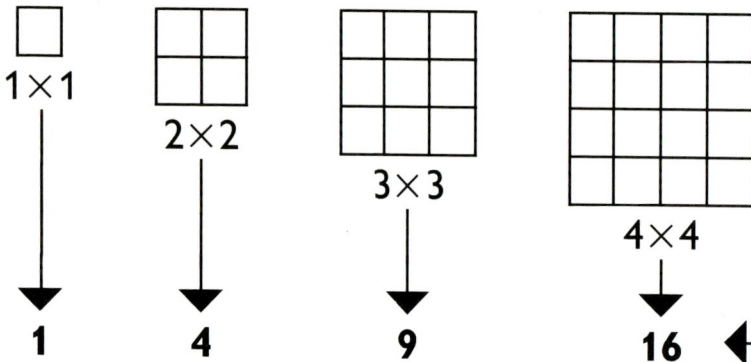

1×1

2×2

3×3

4×4

↓ **1**   ↓ **4**   ↓ **9**   ↓ **16** ←

Number of tiles used

We call numbers like 1, 4, 9, 16, 25, ... SQUARE NUMBERS.

A 5×5 square would need __25__ tiles.
A 6×6 square would need _____ tiles.
A 7×7 square would need _____ tiles.
An 8×8 square would need _____ tiles.
A 9×9 square would need _____ tiles.
A 10×10 square would need _____ tiles.

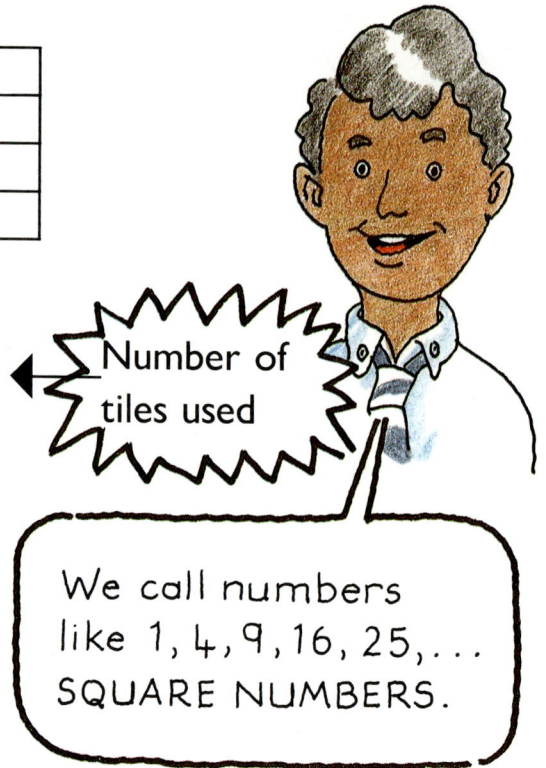

Hamid made some squares using dotty paper.

The first square has 1 dot.
To make the next, 3 more dots.
To make the next, 5 more dots.

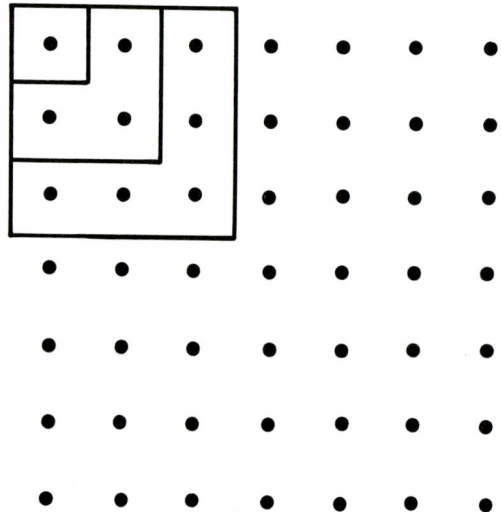

$1 = 1$

$1 + 3 = 4$

$1 + 3 + 5 =$ _____

$1 + 3 + 5 + 7 =$ _____

$1 + 3 + 5 + 7 + 9 =$ _____

$1 + 3 + 5 + 7 + 9 + 11 =$ _____

$1 + 3 + 5 + 7 + 9 + 11 + 13 =$ _____

▶ Finish Hamid's drawing and fill in the numbers.
▶ What sort of numbers did you add together? _____
▶ What sort of numbers are your totals? _____

Hamid wrote the numbers from 1 to 100 on squared paper.

I've written the numbers in a SPIRAL, starting in the middle.

▶ Trace Hamid's **spiral** with your finger, starting from 1.

▶ Colour in all the **square numbers** in Hamid's drawing.

73	74	75	76	77	78	79	80	81	82
72	43	44	45	46	47	48	49	50	83
71	42	21	22	23	24	25	26	51	84
70	41	20	7	8	9	10	27	52	85
69	40	19	6	1	2	11	28	53	86
68	39	18	5	4	3	12	29	54	87
67	38	17	16	15	14	13	30	55	88
66	37	36	35	34	33	32	31	56	89
65	64	63	62	61	60	59	58	57	90
100	99	98	97	96	95	94	93	92	91

▶ Can you spot a pattern in the squares you have coloured? _____

▶ Describe the pattern. _____

_____

21

You will need coloured pencils or pens to show the patterns.

1	2	3	4	5	6	7	8	9	10
11	12	13	14	15	16	17	18	19	20
21	22	23	24	25	26	27	28	29	30
31	32	33	34	35	36	37	38	39	40
41	42	43	44	45	46	47	48	49	50
51	52	53	54	55	56	57	58	59	60
61	62	63	64	65	66	67	68	69	70
71	72	73	74	75	76	77	78	79	80
81	82	83	84	85	86	87	88	89	90
91	92	93	94	95	96	97	98	99	100

▶ Do these:

1 Count in twos and draw a ◯.
So . . . 1 ② 3 ④ and so on. How many ◯s? _____

2 Count in threes and draw a ☐.
So . . . 1   2   ③   4   5   ⑥   and so on. How many ☐s? _____

3 Count in fives and draw a ✗.
So . . . how many multiples of five? _____

4 Count in tens and draw a ✛.
So . . . how many multiples of ten? _____

How many numbers have a
O, ☐, X and + ?

_____

This is a multiplication square. Can you fill in the blanks?

×	1	2	3	4	5	
1					5	
2		4				
3				12		
4	4					
5			15			

×	1	2	3	4	5	6	7	8	9	10
1	1	2	3	4	5	6	7	8	9	10
2		4	6	8	10	12	14	16	18	20
3		6	9	12	15	18	21	24	27	30
4				16	20	24	28	32	36	40
5					25	30	35	40	45	50
6		12				36	42	48	54	60
7							49	56	63	70
8				32				64	72	80
9						54			81	90
10			30							100

Here is another multiplication square. Half is already filled in. Can you fill in the rest?

▶ Now find these multiples:

1 Multiples of five between 20 and 50.

2 Multiples of four between 12 and 36.

3 Multiples of three between 6 and 24.

Going places

We can see where we live. It is marked on this map.

Where do you live?

If it is not marked already, put a dot to show where it is.

Glasgow
Edinburgh
Carlisle
Leeds
Hull
Liverpool
Norwich
Oxford
Cardiff
London
Exeter

This is a distance chart to show how far one place is from another.

It is 126 miles from Liverpool to Carlisle.

Distance chart (diagonal headings, top to bottom): Glasgow, Edinburgh, Carlisle, Hull, Leeds, Liverpool, Norwich, Oxford, Cardiff, Exeter, LONDON

Edinburgh–Glasgow	45
	98 95
	150 236 245
	59 122 206 215
	74 126 126 225 221
	234 175 189 284 370 379
	142 167 170 192 261 362 357
	106 251 202 236 254 296 395 394
	116 151 293 253 287 307 347 446 442
	172 153 56 115 211 194 206 307 405 402

It is 287 miles from Leeds to Exeter.

▶ How far is it from:

   1 Cardiff to Edinburgh? _____

   2 Oxford to Hull? _____

   3 Carlisle to Exeter? _____

▶ Which places are:

1 446 miles apart? _____ and _____

2 59 miles apart? _____ and _____

3 211 miles apart? _____ and _____

▶ Now think of your own questions to ask your family and friends.

13 Boxed in

Find the shapes which can be folded to make a box without a lid like this one.

▶ Copy the square shapes onto paper or card. Make them bigger so they will be easier to handle.

Tick the ones which will make an open box.

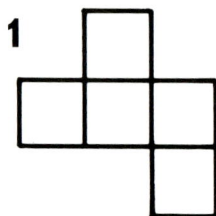

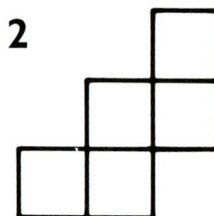

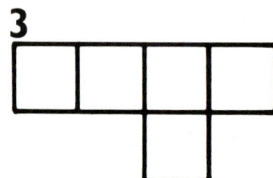

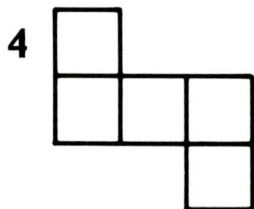

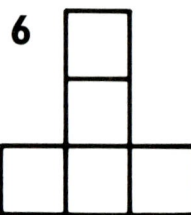

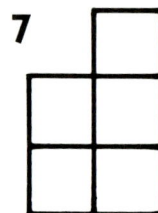

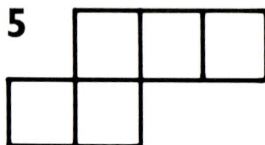

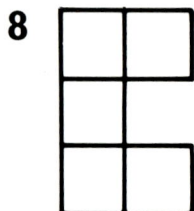

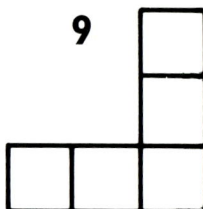

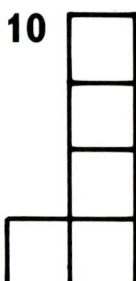

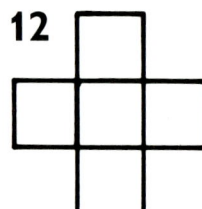

1

2

3

4

5

6

7

8

9

10

11

12

Now choose one of your shapes with a ✓ beside it.
See where you could put a sixth square to make a lid for your box.

There are four places for a lid on this shape.

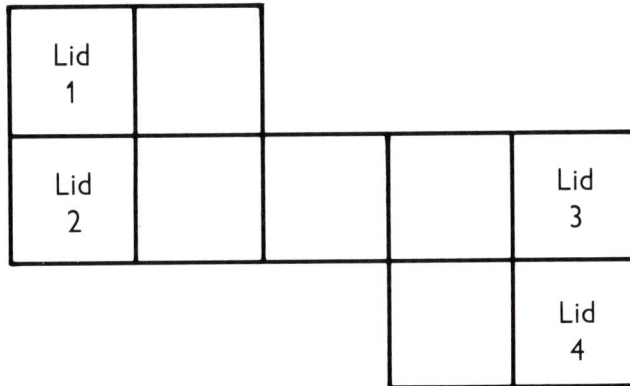

Lid 1	
Lid 2	

	Lid 3
	Lid 4

▶ Draw yours here.

Are there always four places for a lid ? Try to find out.

When I have a lot of numbers to add, subtract, multiply and divide, I try to get a <u>rough</u> answer first.

£1.85	let's call it	£2.00
£2.03	let's call it	£2.00
£3.54	let's call it	£3.50
£0.91	let's call it	£1.00
£2.10	let's call it	£2.00
£5.43	let's call it	£5.50

Exact   £15.86 ◄——— **Total** ———► £16.00   Rough

Hm, yes! About £16. That would be useful when you are using a calculator. Let's try these!

£4.83	let's call it	£ _____	£10.01 let's call it	£ _____
£2.15 ——►	£ _____		£ 5.84 ——►	£ _____
£1.57 ——►	£ _____		£ 3.99 ——►	£ _____
£3.48 ——►	£ _____		£ 1.78 ——►	£ _____
£1.99 ——►	£ _____		£12.57 ——►	£ _____

Total   **Total**

Exact   Rough   Exact   Rough

Difference _____   Difference _____

Will that work for other kinds of sums?

Yes, it gives a check to see that you haven't got a stupid answer.

▶ Try these and then check on your calculator.

Calculator check

$19 \times 21 = ?$ Let's call it _____ × _____ = ☐   _____

Difference = ☐

$51 + 69 = ?$ Let's call it _____ + _____ = ☐   _____

Difference = ☐

$103 - 48 = ?$ Let's call it _____ − _____ = ☐   _____

Difference = ☐

$249 - 88 = ?$ Let's call it _____ − _____ = ☐   _____

Difference = ☐

$399 + 26 = ?$ Let's call it _____ + _____ = ☐   _____

Difference = ☐

15 / Domino dodges

> Think of your domino numbers as tens and units.

So [domino 4|5] or [domino 5|4]

would show **4 | 5** or **5 | 4**

▶ Use the set of dominoes you have cut out from the back cover.

▶ Place your domino 'doubles' on the table to match the yellow section below.   Tick when you have done it. _____

▶ Arrange the rest of your dominoes to match the red section.   Tick when you have done it. _____

▶ Now move these dominoes to match the blue section.   Tick when you have done it. _____

6	6	5	6	4	6	3	6	2	6	1	6	0	6
6	5	5	5	4	5	3	5	2	5	1	5	0	5
6	4	5	4	4	4	3	4	2	4	1	4	0	4
6	3	5	3	4	3	3	3	2	3	1	3	0	3
6	2	5	2	4	2	3	2	2	2	1	2	0	2
6	1	5	1	4	1	3	1	2	1	1	1	0	1
6	0	5	0	4	0	3	0	2	0	1	0	0	0

▶ Which numbers from 0 to 66 cannot be shown in this way with your dominoes?

_____

_____

_____

▶ Use only these dominoes:

▶ Place these dominoes on the track below in such a way that the spots on each side of the circles add up to 10.

▶ When you have done it, record your answer on the domino track.

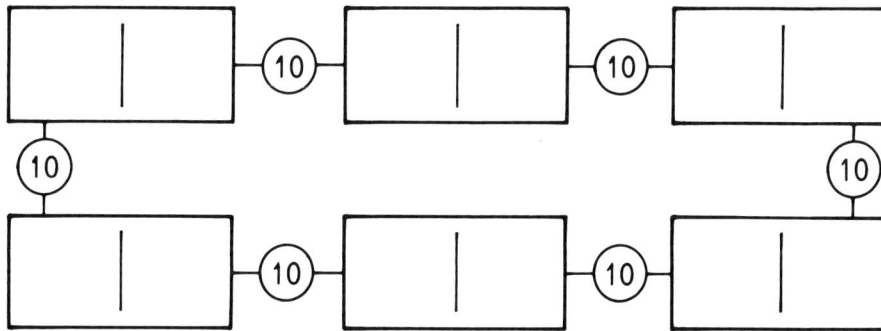

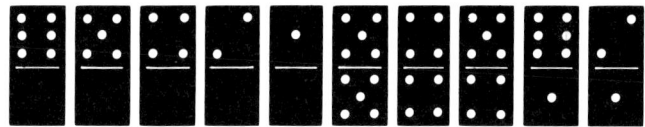

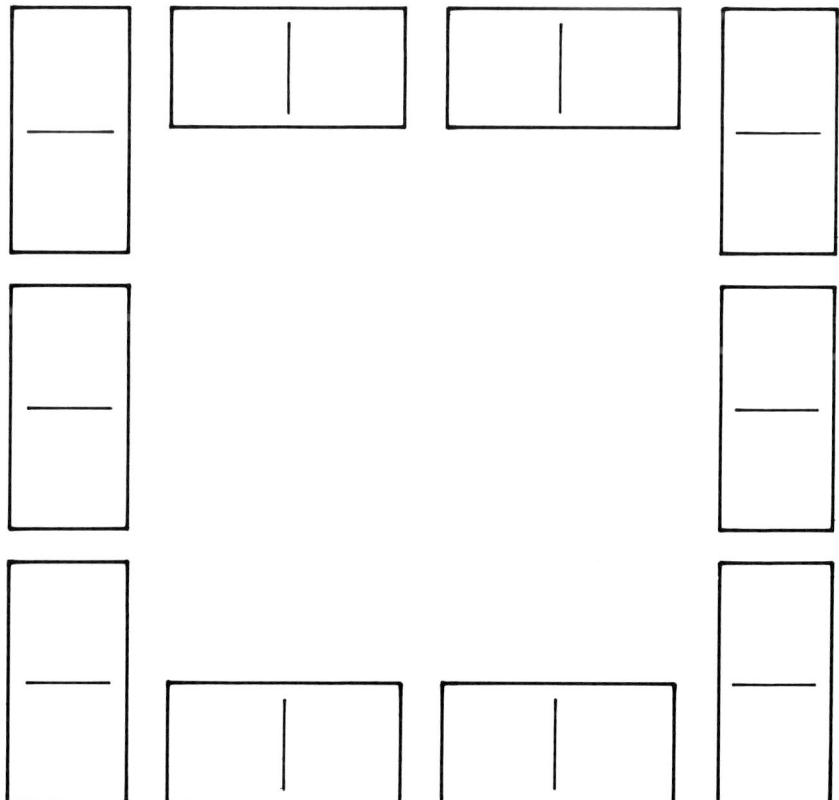

▶ Now use only these dominoes:

▶ Place these dominoes on the track below in such a way that the spots on each side of the square add up to 18.

▶ When you have done it, record your answer on the domino track.

16 Time for tables

Pat and Ruth are in different classes at school.

Here is my lesson timetable.

	9.00	9.30		10.30	10.45		12.00	1.15		2.30	2.45		3.45
MONDAY		NEWS			MATHS			TOPIC			MUSIC+ DRAMA		
TUESDAY	A S S E M B L Y	MATHS	P L A Y T I M E		LIBRARY	L U N C H		GAMES	P L A Y T I M E		TOPIC		
WEDNESDAY		STORY / SCIENCE			SCIENCE			ART+ CRAFT			ART+ CRAFT		
THURSDAY		SWIMMING			LANGUAGE			MATHS			TOPIC		
FRIDAY		LANGUAGE			P.E.			MATHS			PROJECT		

◄——— a.m. ———►◄►——— p.m. ———►

1 What does Pat do on
Wednesday afternoons? _____

2 On which days would Pat have to
take her kit into school? _____

3 When does Pat go swimming?   day _____ time _____

4 What would Pat be doing at
11.00 a.m. on Tuesdays? _____

5 How long does Pat have for lunch? _____

Here is my lesson timetable.

	MON	TUE	WED	THU	FRI
9.00 – 9.30	A	S S	E M	B L	Y
	MATHS	SCIENCE	LANGUAGE	MATHS	SWIMMING
10.30 – 10.45	P L	A Y	T	I M	E
11.30	LANGUAGE	SCIENCE / T.V.	MATHS	MUSIC+ DRAMA	LANGUAGE
12.00 – 1.15		L U	N	C H	
	TOPIC	GAMES	TOPIC	ART+ CRAFT	MATHS
2.30 – 2.45	P L	A Y	T	I M	E
3.15 – 3.45	TOPIC	PROJECT	STORY / P.E.	ART+ CRAFT	LIBRARY

a.m.

p.m.

1 How long does Ruth's story session last on Wednesday afternoons?

_____

2 What would Ruth be doing at 3.20 p.m. on Wednesdays?

_____

3 How long does Ruth spend doing Science each week?

_____

▶ On a scrap of paper design your **ideal** lesson timetable. You can include any lessons you would like, e.g. parachuting, deep sea diving, hot air ballooning, etc.

17 Measuring curves

Tom was trying to measure a winding lane on a map.

I can't do it because my ruler won't bend!

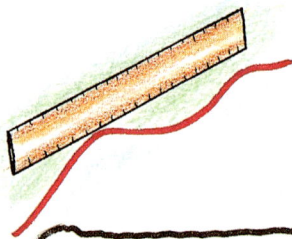

You could use a tape measure on its side.

You could measure it with string.... then measure the string with your ruler.

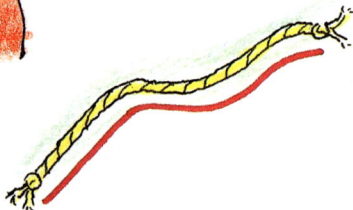

You could measure it with the edge of a strip of paper .... a little bit at a time.

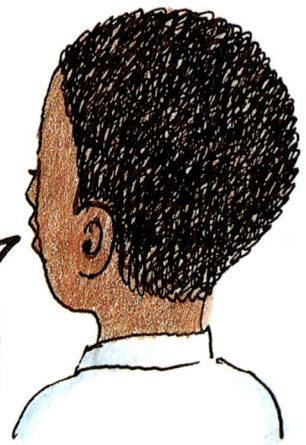

▶ Measure these lines in one of the ways suggested.

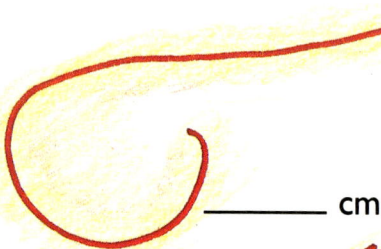

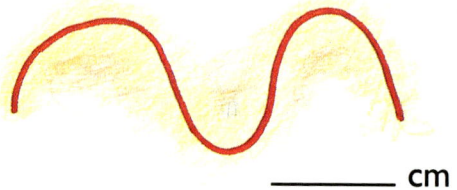

_____ cm

_____ cm

_____ cm

▶ Now measure these.

You can measure them to the nearest centimetre, or, if you prefer, you can be really accurate and measure them in millimetres.

Tom's smile is

_____ wide.

Pat's hair is _____ long.

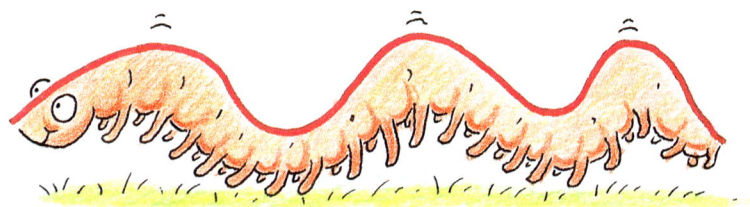

Leon's caterpillar is _____ long.

Mary's pet snake is

_____ long.

18 Domino demons

Ruth and Tom decided to invent a new game of their own, using a set of dominoes.

I know! . . . We'll add up the spots on each domino and collect certain totals each.

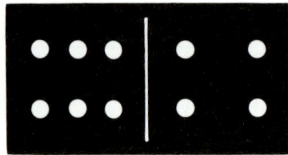

Total 10 →

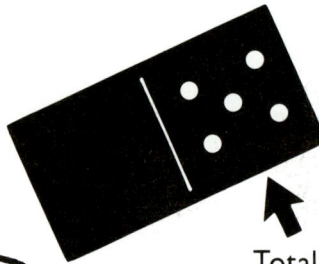

Total 5

Total 6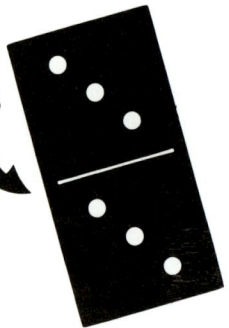

I'll collect the dominoes that total 4, 5, 6, 7, 8 or 9.

. . . and I'll collect the ones that add up to 0, 1, 2, 3, 10, 11 or 12.

I'm collecting SEVEN SETS of dominoes . . . Ruth is only collecting SIX SETS . . . so I'm bound to win!

▶ Sort out your dominoes into sets with the same total.

▶ Use real dominoes or cut out the set from the back cover.

Total 8

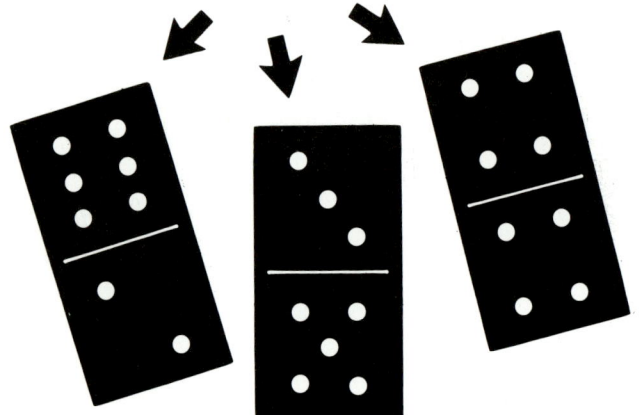

▶ Complete the chart opposite and give it a title.

Title: _____

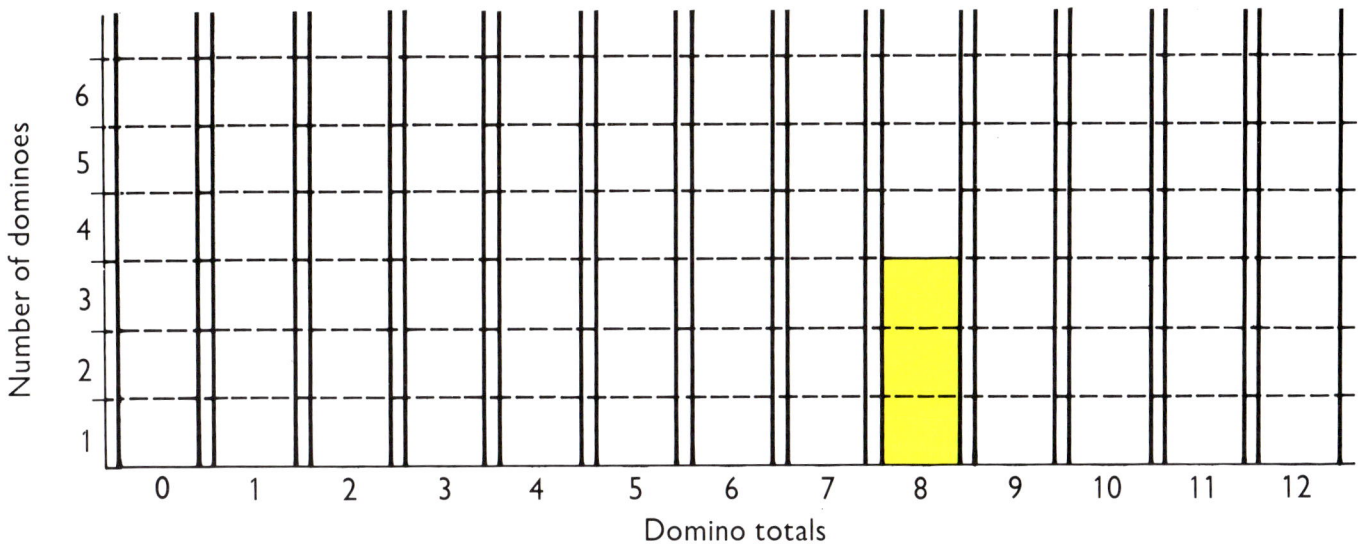

Number of dominoes (y-axis: 1, 2, 3, 4, 5, 6)

Domino totals (x-axis: 0, 1, 2, 3, 4, 5, 6, 7, 8, 9, 10, 11, 12)

Ruth collected the dominoes with totals of 4, 5, 6, 7, 8 and 9.

▶ How many dominoes did she collect? _____

Tom collected the dominoes with totals of 0, 1, 2, 3, 10, 11 and 12.

▶ How many dominoes did he collect? _____

▶ Who won the game? _____

▶ Was the game fair, or was Tom tricked? _____

_____

You could play domino **differences** by subtracting
the spots instead of adding them.

▶ What would be the biggest difference? _____

▶ What would be the smallest difference? _____

▶ Fill in this chart.

0	1	2	3	4	5	6	◀ differences
							◀ number of dominoes

If you could only collect three sets of differences,
which ones would you choose?

_____   _____   _____

37

Can you finish enlarging this funny face? Colour it in when you have finished.

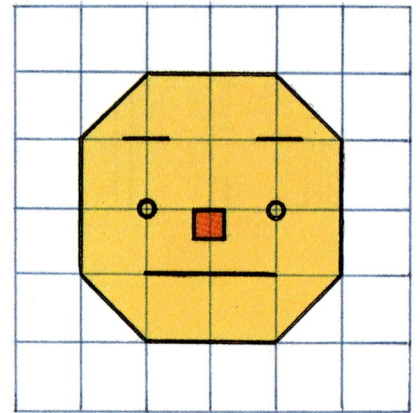

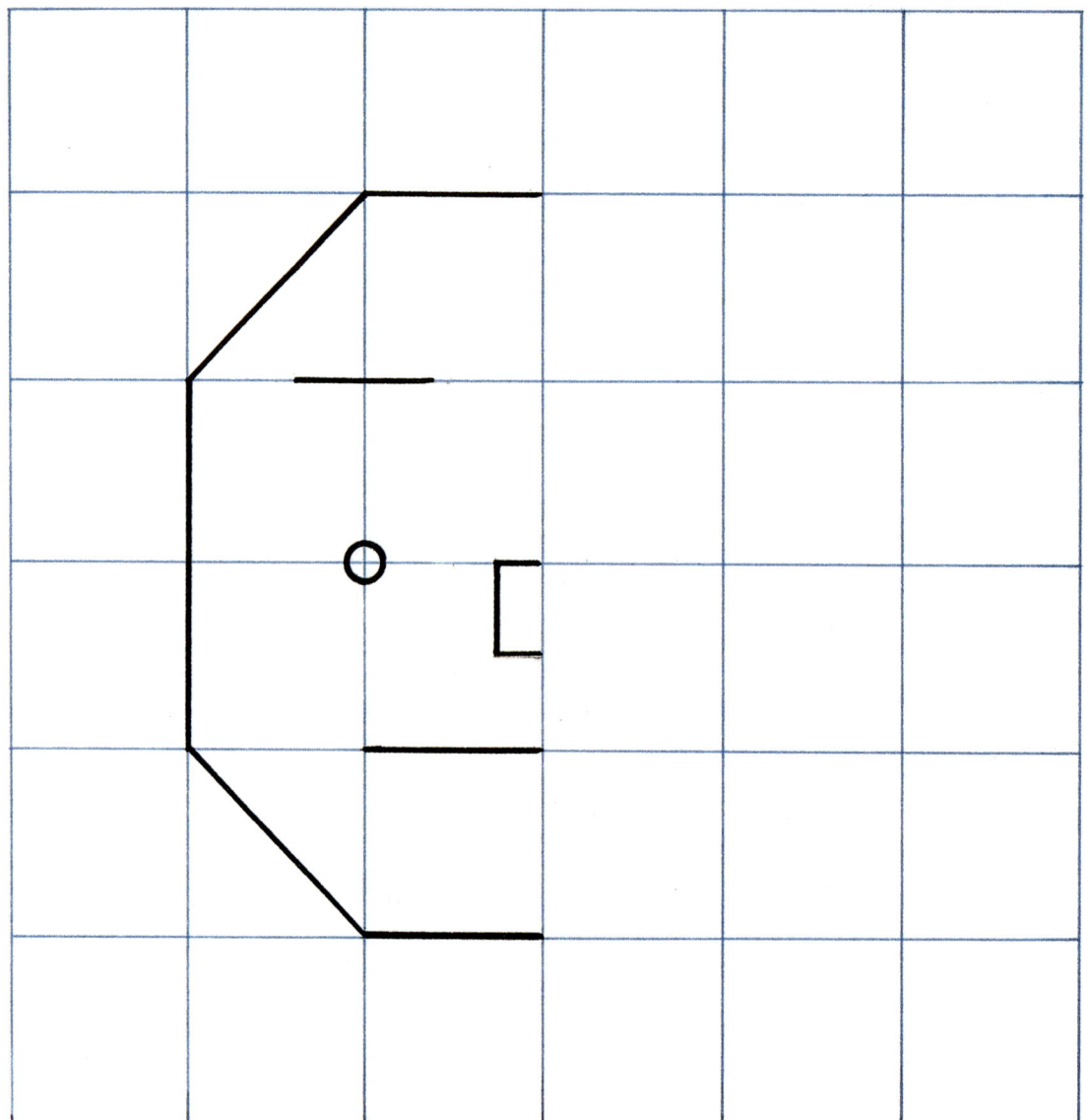

Just look what else you can do to the poor fellow on the opposite page. Finish each picture.

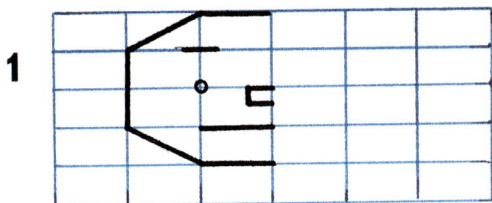

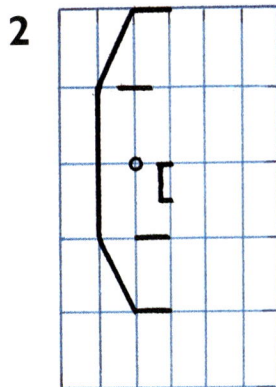

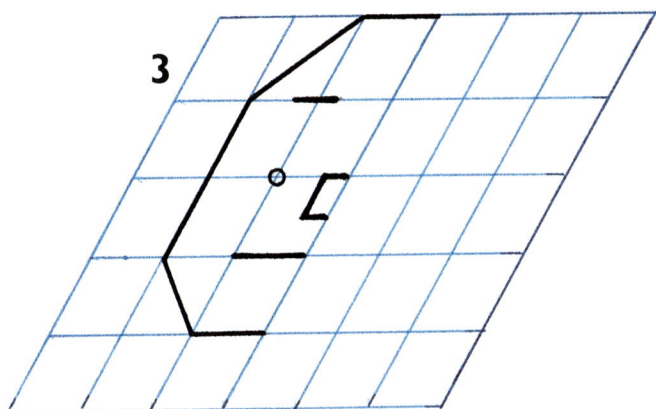

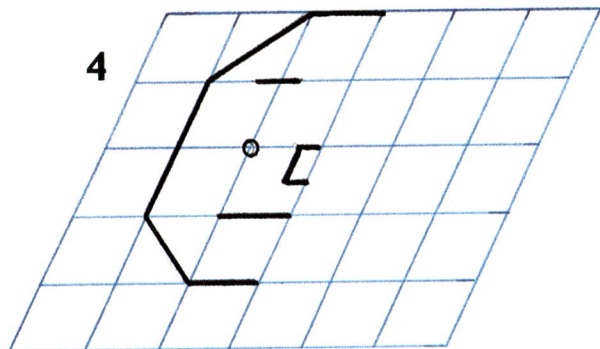

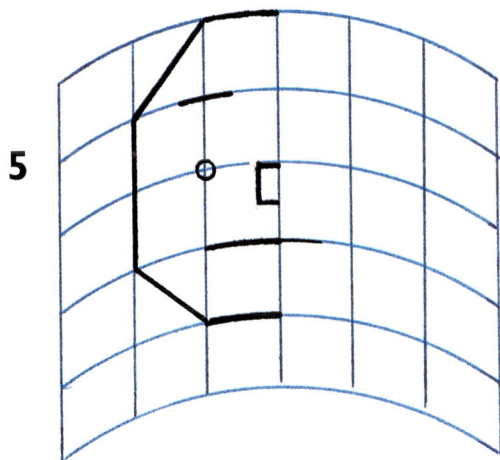

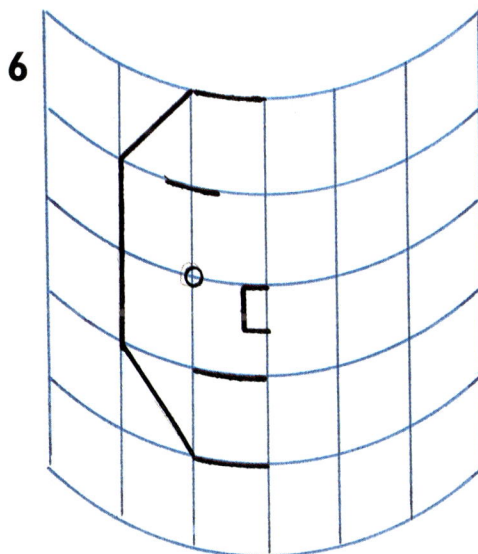

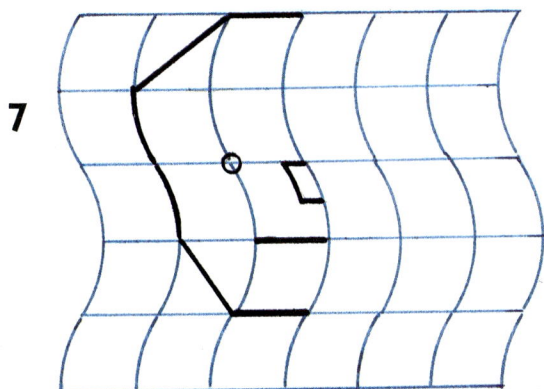

1

2

3

4

5

6

7

I like number ☐ best.

Answers

To Parents:

We have not provided all the answers here. We suggest that activities to be carried out by your child, such as drawing, colouring, etc., should be checked by you. Where calculations are performed by your child, it would be good practice to get him/her to use a calculator to check the answers.

Unit No.	Answers
1	p.2 Head – pentagon, Eyes – pentagon, Nose – rhombus/parallelogram/diamond/quadrilateral, Mouth – square, Neck – square, Skirt – trapezium/quadrilateral, Bow – triangle/equilateral triangle, Hands – hexagon, Shoulders – square, Body – rectangle/oblong, Arms and legs – parallelograms/quadrilaterals; Feet – trapezium/quadrilateral.
2	p.4 **2** 9, **3** 13½, **4** 20, **5** 8½.
3	p.6 **1** 25 km, **2** 32 km, **3** 32 km, **4** 43 km, **5** 63 km. p.7 **1** 5 km, **2** 24 km, **3** 13 km. **1** Sprinton, **2** Runly, **3** Runly.
4	p.8 6, 12, 18, 24, 30, 36, 42, 48, 54, 60. p. 9 Top – five-pointed star; Bottom – ten-pointed star.
5	p.10 **1** 125 cm, **2** 105 cm, **3** Mary, **4** 5 cm.

	Shortest distance	Longest distance
1	4	4
2	6	8
3	8	12
4	10	16
5	12	20
6	14	24

(Unit No. 8)

Unit No.	Answers
10	p.20 36, 49, 64, 81, 100. Consecutive odd numbers. Square numbers. p.21 Pattern is two 'half diagonal' lines.
11	p.22 **1** 50 circles, **2** 33 squares, **3** 20 crosses, **4** 10 pluses. Three numbers have a circle, square, cross and plus around them. They are 30, 60 and 90. p.23 **1** 25, 30, 35, 40, 45; **2** 16, 20, 24, 28, 32; **3** 9, 12, 15, 18, 21.
12	p.25 **1** 395 miles, **2** 192 miles, **3** 347 miles. **1** Exeter and Edinburgh, **2** Leeds and Hull, **3** London and Liverpool.
13	p.26 Shapes which will make an open box: 1, 2, 3, 4, 5, 6, 10 and 12. p.27 yes
14	p.28 Exact totals – £14.02 and £34.19. p.29 Calculator checks – 399, 120, 55, 161, 425.
15	p.30 7, 8, 9, 17, 18, 19, 27, 28, 29, 37, 38, 39, 47, 48, 49, 57, 58, 59.

p.31

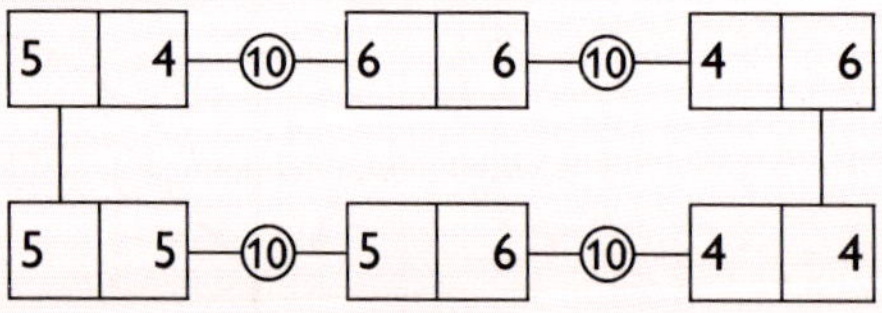

is **one** possible solution.

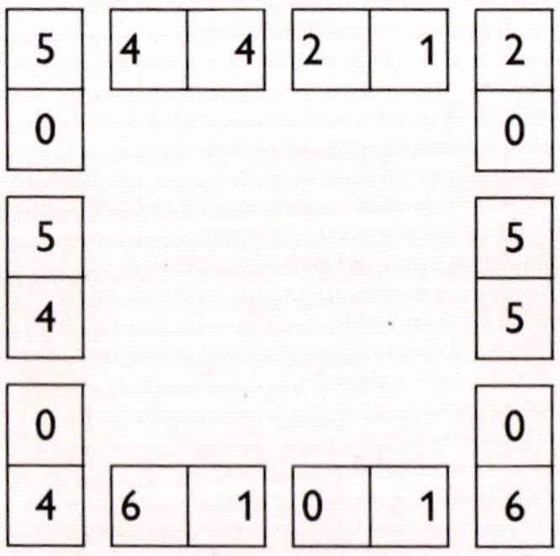

is **one** possible solution.

Unit No.	Answers
16	p.32 **1** Art and craft; **2** Tuesday, Thursday and Friday; **3** Thursday, 9.30 a.m.; **4** Library; **5** 1¼ hours. p.33 **1** ½ hour; **2** P.E.; **3** 1¾ hours.
17	p.34 11 cm, 9½ cm, 13½ cm. p.35 Smile about 6 cm; Caterpillar about 12½ cm; Hair about 17½ cm; Snake about 25 cm.
18	p.37 Ruth 18, Tom 10. Ruth won. Tom was tricked. Biggest difference 6, smallest difference 0.

0	1	2	3	4	5	6
7	6	5	4	3	2	1

Would choose 0, 1 and 2 to collect.